Bible Study Leadership Made Easy

*Lead a women's Bible Study
group with confidence and grace*

MELANIE NEWTON

JOYFUL
WALK
BIBLE
STUDIES

Bible Study Leadership Made Easy: Lead a women's Bible Study group with confidence and grace

© 2025 by Melanie Newton. All rights reserved.

Published by Joyful Walk Ministries. Flower Mound, TX.

ISBN: 979-8-9926517-9-9

For questions about the use of this study guide or for bulk orders, please email us at melanienewton.com/contact.

Cover graphic is a background created by welcomia, accessed at canva.com. Cover design and study layout by Melanie Newton.

Melanie Newton is the author of "Graceful Beginnings" books for anyone new to the Bible and "Joyful Walk Bible Studies" for established Christians. Her mission is to help women learn to study the Bible for themselves and to grow their Bible-teaching skills to lead others on a joyful walk with Jesus.

Joyful Walk Bible Studies are grace-based studies for women of all ages. Each study guide follows the inductive method of Bible Study (observation, interpretation, application) in a warm and inviting format.

We pray that you will find *Bible Study Leadership Made Easy* a resource that God will use to strengthen you in your faith walk with God and your ministry to others.

Christ-Focused • Grace-Based • Bible-Rich

JOYFUL WALK MINISTRIES
FLOWER MOUND, TX

MELANIE NEWTON

Melanie Newton is a Louisiana girl who made the choice to follow Jesus while attending LSU. She and her husband Ron married and moved to Texas for him to attend Dallas Theological Seminary. They stayed in Texas where Ron led a wilderness camping ministry for troubled youth for many years. Ron now helps corporations with their challenging employees and is the author of the top-rated business book, *No Jerks on the Job*.

Melanie jumped into raising three Texas-born children and serving in ministry to women at her church. Through the years, the Lord has given her opportunity to do Bible teaching and to write grace-based Bible studies for women that are now available from her website (melanienewton.com) and on Bible.org. *Graceful Beginnings* books are for anyone new to the Bible. *Joyful Walk Bible Studies* are for maturing Christians.

Melanie is a speaker, author, and trainer with Joyful Walk Ministries. Her mission is to help women learn to study the Bible for themselves and to grow their Bible-teaching skills to lead others. Her heart's desire is to encourage you to have a joyful relationship with Jesus Christ so you are willing to share that experience with others around you.

"Jesus took hold of me in 1972, and I've been on this great adventure ever since. My life is a gift of God, full of blessings in the midst of difficult challenges. The more I have learned and experienced God's absolutely amazing grace, the more I have discovered my faith walk to be a joyful one. I'm still living that joyful walk every day…"

Melanie

OTHER BIBLE STUDIES BY MELANIE NEWTON

All books by *Joyful Walk Ministries* are available as paperbacks and printable / fillable pdfs as well as digital reader versions. Download our catalogue and resources at melanienewton.com.

Graceful Beginnings books for anyone new to the Bible:

A Fresh Start (basics for new Christians)

Painting the Portrait of Jesus (the Gospel of John)

The God You Can Know (the character of God)

Grace Overflowing (an overview of Paul's 13 letters)

The Walk from Fear to Faith (Old Testament women)

Satisfied by His Love (women who knew Jesus)

Seek the Treasure (study of Ephesians)

Pathways to a Joyful Walk (6 pathways to a joy-filled life)

Songs of the Heart That Light My Way (selected Psalms)

Joyful Walk Bible Studies for growing Christians:

Adorn Yourself with Godliness (1 Timothy and Titus, also in Spanish)

Everyday Women, Ever Faithful God (Old Testament women, also in Spanish)

Connecting Faith to Life on Planet Earth (Genesis 1-11; Revelation)

Graceful Living (the essentials for a grace-based Christian life)

Graceful Living Today (a devotional journal for a joyful life)

Healthy Living (Colossians and Philemon)

Heartbreak to Hope (the Gospel of Mark)

Identity: Sticking to Your Faith in a Pull-Apart World (Ezra thru Malachi)

Knowing Jesus, Knowing Joy (Philippians, also in Spanish)

Live Out His Love (New Testament women)

Perspective (1and 2 Thessalonians)

Profiles of Perseverance (Old Testament men, also in Spanish)

Radical Acts (Acts)

Reboot, Renew, Rejoice (1 and 2 Chronicles)

The God-Dependent Woman (2 Corinthians)

To Be Found Faithful (2 Timothy)

Resources for Leading Others

Be a Christ-Focused Small Group Leader (handbook to lead a small group)

Bible Study Leadership Made Easy (handbook to lead a Bible Study group)

Leap into Lifestyle Disciplemaking

Painting the Picture of Jesus (the "I Am's" of Jesus lessons for children)

Teaching Children the God They Can Know (the character of God for children)

Contents

Introduction

I am Melanie Newton, director of Joyful Walk Ministries and author of *Joyful Walk Bible Studies* used by many people worldwide to grow in their faith walk with Jesus Christ.

> My ministry mission is to help women learn how to study the Bible for themselves and grow their Bible-teaching skills to lead others on a joyful walk with Jesus.

Many churches offer Bible studies for women. All you have to do is sign up. But a lot of churches do not offer Bible studies for women because the churches are too small or have no one to lead the way. Starting and leading a Bible Study group in your church or outside of your church ministry structure can be daunting to most women.

Let us start with a few questions that I often get in emails from women:

- Do you want to do a Bible Study and would rather do it in community with other women rather than by yourself?
- Have you been thinking about starting a Bible Study and inviting others to join you but you do not know where to start?
- Are you afraid that you do not know enough of the Bible to lead a Bible Study for a group?
- Does the thought of directing a discussion make your knees tremble?
- Do you have some experience leading a study but you want to get better at doing it?
- Are you wondering how you would lead the discussion when you get together?

I am so glad that you are here right now.

Did you know that *everyone feels inadequate when they start out?* You are **not** alone. I have been where you are. Thankfully, Jesus took me beyond my insecurities. And He will do the same for you In fact, let me share a bit of my story with you.

MY STORY

As a young college student who was a new Christian, I was just learning how to dive into the Bible and find all its treasures. I wanted to share my discoveries with others. But I didn't know how.

Some college friends and I tried a few small study guides, but we just basically read through them. Then, after college, I joined a large women's Bible Study organization where I learned much from my personal study. But when we got together, the discussion leaders had us just take turns reading and answering the questions. There wasn't a lot of enthusiasm.

There had to be a better way to make Bible Studies come alive for people so they would want to soak it up like I did. Sharing what you learn from your personal Bible Study should be fun, not boring! After all, it is God's Word. In it, we find His immense love for us expressed in His grace toward us.

Fast forward a few years. Our family was led by the Lord to a church where the women's Bible Study group wrote its own lessons. As a result, the enthusiasm of the women was sky high. The leaders met together to share what they were learning on their own from the study. And that enthusiasm carried over to the group discussion. It was full of joy, and it was fun!

As I participated in various small groups, watching other joyful women lead the Bible Study discussions, I thought, "I could do this too."

Then, they asked me to be a leader, and it took off for me! Many of the Bible Studies on my website came from that time, a time that stimulated my joyful walk with Jesus.

Through the encouragement of others, I was able to step above my insecurities and learn how to lead a Bible Study discussion with confidence and grace. That changed my life!

ENCOURAGING YOU

That is why I am here to help you through this handbook *"Bible Study Leadership Made Easy."* Using this book, you will learn how to lead a study with confidence and grace.

Bible Study Leadership Made Easy is designed to get you moving forward as a new Bible Study leader or to give you some extra help if you are an experienced leader.

Through this book, you will learn how to put together a Bible Study group, to choose a good study for your group, and how to make a lesson plan for leading the discussion. We will also address some common challenges that come with leading a Bible Study.

By sharing with you some insights that have helped me over the years, I want to help **you** gain confidence to lead your group. You can use these suggestions whether you use one of my *Joyful Walk Bible Study* guides or someone else's.

Are you ready for this learning adventure? Let's get started.

BIBLE STUDY LEADERSHIP MADE EASY VIDEOS

Go to my YouTube channel @joyfulwalking and look for the playlist "Bible Study Leadership Made Easy." These 12 videos cover much of the same information as in this handbook. Checklists referenced in the videos closely match the checklists and worksheets included in this *Bible Study Leadership Made Easy* handbook.

Chapter 1: Begin the Adventure — Just Say Yes!

Leading a Bible Study group is an adventure with Jesus in many ways. And He may be prompting you to start that adventure now. Or you may have tried leading a Bible Study and want to get better at doing it. Whether it is for an existing group or for a new group, I want to start with this—you can lead a Bible Study by faith in the One who is guiding you.

YOU CAN LEAD A BIBLE STUDY BY FAITH

Faith is the essential component of the Christian life. Followers of Jesus are to live every day by faith. That is what Paul is communicating to us in Galatians.

> *I have been crucified with Christ and I no longer live, but Christ lives in me. The life I now live in the body, I **LIVE BY FAITH** in the Son of God, who loved me and gave Himself for me. (Galatians 2:20)*

The life you and I live every day is by faith in the Son of God—Jesus Himself.

I love how a Bible teacher I once heard put it:

> Jesus Christ gave His life for you, so that He could give His life to you, so that He could live His life through you. (Ian Thomas, The Saving Life of Christ)

If the Lord is prompting you to lead a Bible Study, just say, "Yes, I will do this, Lord. Please help me." Jesus is with you every step of the way.

What does that mean? By faith, you can lead a Bible Study....

- Any place—church, neighborhood, community, or workplace.
- At any age or stage of life—single, married, widowed, with or without children, working outside the home, working inside the home. Someone around you needs to know Jesus or to know Him better through studying the Bible.
- With any size group—large or small.
- Whether you have been studying the Bible for two years or doing it for decades. Share what you know and what you are learning.

You can do this by faith because whatever Jesus calls you to do, He enables you to do through His Spirit. You can lead a Bible Study not because you are so great or smart or have been a Christian a long time or know the Bible really well. You can do this because Jesus is the one who enables you to do it. Say "yes" and jump in with both feet. **Step out in faith!**

LEADING A BIBLE STUDY IS GOOD FOR YOU

Leading a Bible Study can be one of the greatest adventures you have ever tried. And it is good for you. There are benefits for you when you say yes to leading a Bible Study. What are those benefits?

Leading a Bible Study presses you to grow and learn for yourself. You always learn more when you prepare to help someone else grow in their faith. That is great motivation. You may have already recognized that to be true in your own experience.

Leading a Bible Study teaches you how to depend on Jesus Christ more than yourself: Our God wants us to rely more on Him than relying on ourselves. And whatever leads you to depend on Him is a good thing for you. We are to live by faith in Him and let Him live His life through us (remember Galatians 2:20).

Yes. I know that you are already thinking the "What if such and such happens" and "Yes, but I don't know how to do whatever." You are not alone. Most people who are leading Bible studies today started out with those same feelings of insecurity and hesitation that you are feeling. I did. That is a good thing. Actually, it is a great thing. Remember why? Whatever forces you to depend on Jesus more that yourself is great for you.

TRUST JESUS WITH YOUR INSECURITIES

Give your insecurities to Jesus. He is the one who makes us able to do everything in the Christian life. That includes leading a Bible Study. You are simply to obey Him and trust His Spirit to work through you.

You know what? Being scared is a good thing because you and I will rely on Him more. It is good to say, "Lord, I can't do this on my own, but you can in me and through me. I will trust you with this." And then, watch what He does! Give Him your insecurities. Go ahead, begin the adventure.

Remember these truths:

- You can lead a Bible Study because Jesus makes you able to do so.
- Leading a Bible Study benefits you because it presses you to grow and depend on Jesus more than on yourself.
- You can trust Jesus with your insecurities.

You can do this by faith. Just say, "Yes."

REFLECT AND RESPOND

Review what you learned in this chapter. Then, do this:

What are your insecurities and concerns about leading a Bible Study? List them below:

Give them to Jesus. Consider saying, "Yes, Lord. I will trust you with these." Then, watch what He does!

The next step is to start a Bible Study group if you do not already have one. Get ideas for doing this in Chapter 2.

If you are already leading a group and need to choose what you will study, skip to Chapter 3.

GO AHEAD AND BEGIN THE ADVENTURE!

Chapter 2: Start a Bible Study Group

Starting and leading a Bible Study can be one of the greatest adventures you have ever tried. And it is good for you. So give your insecurities to Jesus. He is the one who makes you able to do everything in the Christian life, and that includes starting a Bible Study. You are simply to obey Him and trust His Spirit to work through you. Being scared is a good thing because you will rely on Him more. You can be confident that Jesus is with you every step of the way. Step out in faith. Say "yes" to Jesus and jump in with both feet.

You will find suggestions in this chapter about starting a new Bible Study group for women.

GETTING STARTED

Start with prayer

Like anything else in the Christian life, start with prayer. Talk it over with Jesus. Let Him know of your desire to start a Bible Study group. Ask Him to help you discern all the details—when and where to meet, whom to invite, and what you should study.

Consider whom to invite

Consider ways to invite women to join you for a study. This is easier now with available social media platforms and email.

- You can personally invite neighbors, coworkers, or church friends.

- You can put an invitation on Facebook or other group site and see who responds. This works well for local groups that meet in person as well as groups that meet online through Zoom or other apps. One member of our Joyful Walk Community did that and found a large number of women in her remote area who wanted to do a Bible Study with her through a Facebook Group, occasionally meeting together at a local coffee shop.

- Maybe you have some mommy friends who need to have some adult discussion. I know a group of women who get together for Bible Study right after they drop their children off at school in the morning.

- Consider inviting some coworkers to join you during your lunch break. One friend of mind did that. She and about 5 coworkers met for 6-8 weeks during the lunch hour. It built some community among employees who had not previously known about each other's faith. The Navigators ministry calls these "Learning Communities." I like that phrase.

- Will your invites go to women who are mostly seasoned Bible students or new to the Bible?

Decide when to meet

- What would be the best time? Look at the time that works for you and your group—morning, lunch, afternoon, evening. You might need to meet early in the morning before school or work or on Saturday mornings. Offer a "lunch-and-learn" Bible Study for your coworkers.

- How long can your group meet? 1 hour, 1½ hours, 2 hours? Whatever works for you and for those you invite. Go for it.

- How often? You don't have to meet every week. I know of several groups of friends who meet only twice a month for Bible Study. It does help to not go too long between meetings, though. You can lose consistency in thought if too much time passes. At least, I do!

- Will you be meeting online? Be conscious of time zones and how that might affect those joining your group from other locations. I led an online study that included women from the East Coast, the West Coast, and Asia. It was hard to choose a time that would be useful to all of them. And I had to consider how the changes to / from Daylight Savings Time would affect the women.

Find a place to meet

Try to find a place that is large enough and will allow the women to hear and see each other.

- In a home: Women love meeting in homes for Bible Study. There is something about a home that encourages women to get to know one another and open up with sharing about their lives. If you are leading the lessons, we recommend that you ask someone else to host the group. Some women love doing that and have enough room to accommodate the size of your group.

- Restaurants: The problem with restaurants is that they can be noisy and awkward. You want to be able to hear and see one another. Long tables make that difficult. But some restaurants have side rooms you can reserve or outside patios that work well.

- In a church building: Meeting at a room in your church might be the most convenient place, especially if you like to know you will always have a place to meet away from crowds! But that depends on the openness of your church to have outside groups using the building. Remember that you want everyone to be able to hear and see each other.

- At work: Is there a meeting room in your office area that you could use? Some buildings have conference rooms that can be reserved or other meeting rooms available for employees to gather before work or at lunch.

The possibilities are endless. I met with a group of ladies in the evening at a coffee shop one summer while sitting outside under the awning. Another group met in the café area of a local grocery store over the lunch hour, drawing in women who work from home in our area.

You can try different days, times, and places until you find something that works well for your group.

Choose a Bible Study guide

- Follow the recommendations in Chapter 3 to help you choose a quality Bible Study guide based on your interest, the group's Bible Study experience, and your available group time.

- Determine how to get the Bible Study materials: download and print for all the group members, order books for the group members, or tell the women how to order their own books.

Set a start date and invite others to join you

Set a start date, notify those you are inviting, and tell them how to get the study materials. If available, you can download and print a copy for each person. You can order books for all the group members to have on hand the first time you meet. Or you can direct the group members how to order their own books.

RECAP

In this chapter, you learned how to start a Bible Study group. In Chapter 3, we will cover choosing the right study for your group.

USE THE "START A BIBLE STUDY GROUP" CHECKLIST ON THE NEXT PAGE TO HELP PLAN YOUR NEW GROUP.

"Start a Bible Study Group" checklist

Permission is granted to make copies of this checklist as needed.

Start with prayer

Talk it over with Jesus. Let Him know of your desire to start a Bible Study group. Ask Him to help you discern all the details—when and where to meet, whom to invite, and what you should study. Depend on Him to show you what to do. He is faithful!

Consider whom to invite

✓ Whom will you invite?

✓ How will you invite them?

Decide when to meet

✓ What would be the best time for you and for those you invite?

✓ How long can your group meet each time?

✓ How often will you meet?

Find a place to meet

✓ Where will you meet?

✓ Do you need to reserve a room based on your schedule?

Choose a Bible Study Guide

✓ Will your group be mostly those new to the Bible or those with Bible Study experience?

✓ Choose a quality Bible Study guide based on your interest, the group's Bible Study experience, and your available group time. See Chapter 3.

✓ How will you get the Bible Study materials? Download and print for all the group members, order books for the group members, or tell the women how to order their own books.

Set a start date and invite others to join you

WOOHOO! THE ADVENTURE BEGINS!

Chapter 3: Choosing a Bible Study for Your Group

Choosing a quality Bible Study guide can make your experience at leading either a great one or a frustrating one. This is especially true if you are leading the lessons. Over the years, I have learned some valuable lessons about choosing a Bible Study for a group. In this chapter, I will share that with you.

TYPES OF BIBLE STUDIES

There are two methods of Bible Study —inductive and deductive. So, let me explain the difference.

Inductive Method

The inductive method follows three steps: observation, interpretation and application. The process is more easily understood by answering three questions:

- What does the passage say? (Observation: what it says)
- What does it mean? (Interpretation: the author's intended meaning for him and the intended audience)
- How does this apply to me today? (Application: making it personal)

This is the best way to study the Bible to make sure you are getting biblical truth. Look at what's there. Learn what it means and teaches you. Then, live it out in your life.

The Deductive Method

The deductive method starts with a topic or theme then selectively chooses Bible verses to "prove" whatever the author wants to prove, especially if it is a current fad or cultural position. Many topical studies use the deductive method. For example, you want to see what the Bible teaches about anger. So your Bible Study guide has you look up the verses that deal with anger and then you make applications from them. Topical studies can be valuable for us when we are wanting to learn about some aspect of the Christian life in particular. But I have two cautions about this method of Bible Study:

Caution #1: This method can be used to selectively choose Bible verses to prove anything that someone wants to prove.

> For example, someone could write a Bible Study with the premise that God wants you to be happy and not suffer and then select verses that talk about God wanting to make you happy and prosperous to prove that point.

Caution #2: This method feeds the "look-imagine-see" way of looking at the Bible, which leads to error. Let me explain.

> Someone looks at a verse or passage, imagines what they want it to say, and then "sees" in their mind what they have imagined through twisting word meanings and interpretations. Many types of false teaching through the years have started with this kind of "look-imagine-see" process. Avoid that!

The deductive process is an unreliable method for studying the Bible. Sometimes popular topics use this method. Just beware.

Check the front of the study guide to see if it says it follows the inductive process. Follow this method if you are creating your own study as well. All *Joyful Walk Bible Studies* are "Inductive Bible Studies" and can be trusted to lead you to biblical truth.

BIBLE STUDY FORMATS

You generally have three options for studies:

1. Printed Bible Study guide without associated videos.

2. Printed Bible Study guide with associated videos.

3. Bible book or topic without a printed study guide—unscripted studies.

When I say "Bible Study" I am talking about covering portions of the Bible (whole books or sections of the Bible) in an organized fashion. Printed Bible Study guides are scripted studies, written out for you. They are sometimes called workbooks. In the following recommendations, I will refer to them as Bible Study guides. Most of the recommendations apply to reading and discussing the Bible without a printed study guide.

Be aware of this: Popular books that contain some Bible verses in them are **not** Bible studies, even if they have discussion guides in them. Those can be valuable learning tools but not as a Bible Study.

CHOOSING THE BIBLE STUDY FOR YOUR GROUP

Start with prayer

Ask Jesus to help you to choose a quality Bible Study for your group. Depend on Him to show you what to do. He is faithful!

Consider your familiarity with the Bible as well as the group members

- *Are you new at leading a Bible Study lesson?* Choose a Bible Study guide that is short and easy to lead. Look at the format of the study. Can the questions be used as a guide for leading the discussion? A well-written Bible Study guide will make it easier for you to learn how to lead a Bible Study lesson.

- *Are most of the women in your group new to the Bible?* Start with a study of Jesus Christ from the gospels. Look for a Bible Study designed for those who are new to the Bible or beginners at studying the Bible. You want basic lessons with simple questions and applications using terms that are easy-to-understand for beginners. Our "Graceful Beginnings" studies work well for beginners, fit well in a limited discussion time of an hour or less, and are easy to lead. We offer several that focus on who Christ is and how to have a relationship with Him.

- *Do most of the women in your group already have some Bible Study experience?* You have lots of options. Be sure your choice uses the "Inductive" process as described above. Bible studies designed for Christians who already have some experience studying the Bible have longer lessons with questions that assume you have a working knowledge of the Bible. Once again, make sure they are Christ-focused more than author-focused.

- *Is your group mixed regarding Bible Study experience?* Choose a study for the inexperienced ones and communicate to the experienced ones that they will learn something new. The Bible is living and relevant.

Consider the format that works best for your group

When I say "Bible Study" I am talking about covering portions of the Bible (whole books or sections of the Bible) in an organized fashion. Any "Bible Study" should help you learn by reading the Bible verses then answering specific questions based on what you just read. As mentioned above, your general choices are printed studies with or without videos and unscripted studies that you design yourself.

- *Printed Bible Studies:* Printed Bible Study guides are scripted studies, written out for you. They are sometimes called workbooks. Make sure the Bible Study you choose focuses more on what you are learning from your study of the Bible passages rather than on reading the author's commentary. Bible Study should always be Christ-focused, not personality-driven or author-focused. The Bible should be your main text. All of our *Joyful Walk Bible Studies* are Bible-rich and Christ-focused with limited commentary. See below for specific recommendations regarding video-driven studies,

- *Unscripted Studies:* If you want to lead a Bible Study discussion by just reading through a book of the Bible and discuss that, I call those unscripted studies. That means you are making up your own questions to discuss with your group. This is easier to do if you are experienced at both studying the Bible and leading a Bible Study discussion. It is harder for someone who is new to leading a Bible Study group. Writing your own study? Make sure they are Bible-rich and Christ-focused more than commentary filled.

- *What about popular books?* Popular books that contain some Bible verses in them are **not** Bible studies, even if they have discussion guides in them. Those can be valuable learning tools but not as a Bible Study.

Choose what interests you and will grow you in your faith

- *Ask yourself what would be the best focus for you in your life right now or for your group.* Consider what you have already studied and what might be the best thing to build onto that. Your passion about the study will motivate you to dig in and learn for yourself. It's important that you feed yourself from the Word of God before you try to lead others in a discussion. Remember one of the benefits of leading a Bible Study is that it presses you to grow and learn for yourself. And the joy of what you are learning will be infectious to those in your group.

- *Choose the study and run with it* rather than try to please everyone in the group. The truth is that will not be able to please everyone. Pray about what is best for the group.

- *For those who have already studied that book of the Bible you chose,* suggest that this is the time for them to help someone else understand it. Remind them that Bible Study in a group is not all about "me." It is about the whole group learning together. The Word of God is alive and active. If she is open to it, she will learn something new.

- *If someone who has been in Bible studies for years complains that the one you chose is too easy,* suggest that she invite a friend or coworker who is new to the Bible to attend this one. Then, she can be the mentor for that person.

Consider how long your group meets and how much of any lesson you can cover

- *Do you have 1½ to 2 hours or more?* You can usually cover one lesson per session without rushing through the lesson.

- *Do you have only an hour or less?* Choose a shorter study or a study that can be divided into two sessions. You don't want to feel rushed trying to get through all of the questions in a short time. The group time should be a learning experience, not just a challenge to get through the lesson.

Ask questions about video-driven studies

Wonderful gifted teachers have made their messages available through Bible studies that have accompanying videos. You can always learn something from gifted Bible teachers. But when it comes to choosing a Bible Study for your group, here are some questions to ask and things to consider before choosing a study that requires watching a video to complete it:

- *Does the study lead everyone to dig into the Bible for themselves to learn?* Look at the personal study portion to see if it covers the passage well. Is it an actual study of the Bible according to the inductive process, or does it contain mostly thought and reflection questions?

- *Can someone learn from the Bible passage through the study without watching the video at all?* If yes, sounds like it might be a good study. If no, avoid it. **The video should be like "icing on the cake" not the cake itself.**

- *Will the cost and access to the videos and books be easily shared by the group members?* Video-driven studies are convenient but can be expensive. You must still purchase a workbook for every participant plus acquire access to the videos. You must depend on technology to work perfectly every time. Will that be a challenge for you? Will it fluster you if showing the video does not work during your group time?

- *Can the group members watch the videos on their own time through an app or website and then share what they learned during group time?* It may be hard to find a video-driven study that can be used in an hour or less during a typical lunch hour at work or during an evening study at the end of a hard work day. The videos are generally too long to allow for much group discussion at all. It is difficult to build community when you are just watching someone else talk. And watching a video together is not a good substitute for interaction within the group. If the group members can watch the videos on their own time through an app or website and then share what they learned during group time, then that study might work. This is the better way when it comes to building community within the time limits that you may have.

- *As leader, will you feel restricted to focus your discussion on whatever is taught in the video?* It is better if you can dig into a lesson yourself then focus on what your particular group needs the most from the study. Again, look at the personal study portion to see if it covers the passage well. Like I said earlier, the video should be like "icing on the cake" not the cake itself.

Yes, leading a group of people through a Bible Study discussion is hard and scary. But that's a good thing because you will depend on Jesus more. Just say, "Lord Jesus, I do not feel confident leading a Bible Study group. But I will let You do that through me. I am willing to learn from You and depend on You as I do this." Then, watch what He does!

RECAP

In this chapter, you learned how to choose a published Bible Study for your group and questions to ask about choosing a study that depends upon watching a video to complete it.

In Chapter 4, we will cover how to prepare to be the discussion leader for your group and what to do on the first day that you meet together.

USE THE "HOW TO CHOOSE A BIBLE STUDY TO LEAD" CHECKLIST ON THE NEXT PAGE TO HELP YOU CHOOSE A BIBLE STUDY TO LEAD FOR YOUR GROUP.

"How to Choose a Bible Study to Lead" checklist

Permission is granted to make copies of this checklist as needed.

Ask Jesus to help you with all of the following steps to choosing a Bible Study for your group. Depend on Him to show you what to do. He is faithful!

Start with prayer

Ask Jesus to help you to choose a quality Bible Study for your group. Depend on Him to show you what to do. He is faithful!

Consider your familiarity with the Bible as well as the group members

✓ Are you new at leading a Bible Study lesson? Choose a Bible Study guide that is short and easy to lead. Can the questions be used as a guide for leading the discussion?

✓ Are most of the women in your group new to the Bible? Start with a study of Jesus from the gospels. Look for lessons with simple questions and applications using terms that are easy-to-understand for beginners.

✓ Do most of the women in your group already have some Bible Study experience? Does your choice use the "Inductive" method? Is it Christ-focused more than author-focused?

✓ Is your group mixed regarding Bible Study experience? Choose a study for the inexperienced ones and communicate to the experienced ones that they will learn something new. The Bible is living and relevant.

Consider the format that works best for your group

✓ *Printed Bible Studies:* Does it focus more on what you are learning from your study of the Bible passages rather than on reading the author's commentary?

✓ *Unscripted Studies:* If you want to lead a Bible Study by just reading through a book of the Bible and discuss that, make sure you stay Bible-rich and Christ-focused more than commentary filled.

✓ Are you drawn to a popular book? Those can be valuable learning tools but not as a Bible Study.

Choose what interests you and will grow you in your faith

✓ Ask yourself what would be the best focus for you in your life right now or for your group. Consider what you have already studied and what might be the best thing to build onto that.

✓ Choose the study and run with it rather than try to please everyone in the group. The truth is that will not be able to please everyone. Pray about what is best for the group.

✓ For those who have already studied that book of the Bible you chose, suggest that this is the time for them to help someone else understand it.

✓ If someone who has been in Bible studies for years complains that the one you chose is too easy, suggest that she invite a friend or coworker who is new to the Bible to attend this one..

Consider how long your group meets and how much of any lesson you can cover

✓ Do you have 1½ to 2 hours or more? You can usually cover one lesson per session.

✓ Do you have only an hour or less? Choose a shorter study or a study that can be divided into two sessions.

Ask questions about video-driven studies

✓ Does the study lead everyone to dig into the Bible for themselves to learn? Is it an actual study of the Bible according to the inductive process, or does it contain mostly thought and reflection questions?

✓ Can someone learn from the Bible passages through the study without watching the video at all? If yes, sounds like it might be a good study. If no, avoid it. **The video should be like "icing on the cake" not the cake itself.**

✓ Will the cost and access to the videos and books be easily shared by the group members? Will showing the video be a challenge for you?

✓ Can the group members watch the videos on their own time through an app or website and then share what they learned during group time? Are the videos too long to allow for much group discussion and community building?

✓ As leader, will you feel restricted to focus your discussion on whatever is taught in the video? It is better if you can dig into a lesson yourself then focus on what your particular group needs the most from the study.

What are your choices?

CHECK OUT ALL OF MELANIE'S BIBLE STUDIES AT MELANIENEWTON.COM/FREE-BIBLE-STUDIES.

Chapter 4: Step Forward as the Leader

You are in the process of learning how to lead a study with confidence & grace. This chapter will answer the questions about what to do when you meet together to begin your chosen Bible Study. Ask Jesus to help you lead a Bible Study group. Depend on Him to show you what to do. He is faithful!

RECOGNIZE THE TWO ROLES OF A BIBLE STUDY GROUP LEADER

There are two roles of a Bible Study group leader. You begin both of those roles the first time you get together.

Role #1: Content Guardian

A guardian is a custodian, a keeper, someone who maintains control of something important. For a Bible Study, the "something important" is the truth from God's Word and handling it correctly. As Content Guardian for your group, you have the authority to control the content of the Bible Study discussion. You guard how the truth from God's Word is presented and received.

Role #2: Community Builder

Community within your group is built around your study of God's Word together and how you are each applying it to your life. As Community Builder for your group, you manage the group interaction to help them love one another well.

Those two roles are totally interlinked. If you discuss great content without building community, the group will not gel. Yet, while group community is getting established, the members depend upon you to make sure the content of the discussion stays on track and is fruitful. There must be a healthy balance.

FIRST DAY YOUR GROUP MEETS

You as the leader set the tone for both of those roles the first time you get together. It's important that you make a positive first impression with your group. You set the tone for your role as leader the first time you get together. What would that look like?

Start with prayer

Pray for your group members that their hearts and minds would be open to whatever Jesus wants to teach them through the study and to learn how to love one another well.

Make a positive first impression as "Community Builder"

It is important that you make a positive first impression with your group.

- *Sit so that you face the entrance to the room.* Whether you are in a small room or large one, place yourself so that you can see the entrance that your group members will likely use to join your group. This way whenever someone comes, you can quickly give a welcome smile and even a wave to let them know you are happy to see them. Do this all the time, not just the first day.

- *Sit so that everyone can see and hear you and, if possible, see each other.* Make adjustments to chairs and tables to make this happen.

- *Introduce yourself and start with 1-2 "get acquainted" questions that everyone would have in common.* For example: Share your name, what brought you to this study, how long have you lived in the area, favorite color to wear, or favorite flower—just generic questions. If you have a mixed group of women (married / single / working / stay-at-home), it is best to not start with "tell us about your family" or "tell us about your job." You can share about those later as you get to know one another better.

For an in-person group, make this a "Whoever wants to go next" activity. Don't call on anyone or go around the group if everyone is new. You will build community more effectively if you let people respond when they feel ready to do so. Just ask, "Who wants to go next?"

For an online group, I usually start, then I call on individual women to share. That avoids time delay from internet connections.

Confirm communication details and schedule.

- *Find out the best way to communicate with each one.* Do they respond better to a text, email, FB messenger, phone call, or other? Make note of their responses. Give everyone your contact information, and get their contact information if you don't already have it. Give your group permission to contact you if they do not understand what a question is asking.

- *Schedule and start / end time:* It is a good idea to give them a schedule so they will know what lesson will be discussed on which date.

  Tell them when you will start the group discussion so they will know (at official start time, 5 minutes later, other). And be faithful about this. Set an alarm on your phone. For example, if your official time is 10am-12pm. If you say you will start at 10:05, then begin something at 10:05—a get acquainted question related to the lesson, report on answered prayer, or the beginning of the lesson. Anyone who arrives late can join right in. You can tell women they can come early and visit. But they need to know you will be faithful to start on time.

  Tell them when you will end the group discussion and prayer. Be faithful to end on time as well.

- *Sharing prayer requests:* Talk about how you will share prayer requests.

  Some groups have time to let all members share their requests in the group time. Hand out blank cards and having them write their requests on cards helps.

  Another idea is to have the women write their requests on the cards, hand them to one person to read aloud who also prays the requests. Emailing them to group members is a valuable way to build community within the group. If time, break up into groups of 2-3 and pray each other's requests. Then, give them to anyone who will be emailing them to the whole group.

  Be sure to tell them to mark "Private" on anything not meant to be shared via email or aloud. And pay attention to this!

Confirm all have Bibles and study guides.

- *Make sure everyone has a Bible or Bible app* (suggest a good one that is easy to use).

- *Ask if anyone is new to studying the Bible.* This is important information for you as a leader. Make sure they have a Bible and make a note to yourself that that person might need help learning how to find Bible verses and answer questions. I have learned not to assume that people know how to do that.

- *Make sure everyone has a Bible Study book or knows where to get one.* If you have all the books, remember to get a book to anyone who misses the first day so she can do the lesson before the next meeting. If you have individuals buy books, try to find a way to help someone pay for a book if they aren't able to do so on their own. If you are not using a study guide, let them know what to expect.

- *Ask if they are okay with reading aloud paragraphs and Bible verses.* Find out who is not comfortable reading aloud and remember not to call on her to read a Bible verse or paragraph in the book. If your group is experienced, you may ask them to read a question and answer it.

Introduce the study as the "CONTENT GUARDIAN"

As you introduce the study, you want to do so in a way that generate interest in the study. This is where your excitement about doing the study really shines through.

- *Look at the "Contents" page to create interest in the study.* Lesson titles often give clues as to what they will learn in that lesson.

- *Will you do one lesson per group time or take two sessions to do one lesson?* Make sure they understand this. Consider providing a schedule with the dates and lessons to be covered to keep everyone on track.

Scan the "Introduction" section.

Most Bible Study guides have some kind of introduction or overview before the lessons begin. Every *Joyful Walk Bible Study* has an Introduction section. This is a good thing to cover together on your first day. The following is based on what is found at the beginning of most *Joyful Walk Bible Studies*.

- *Talk about the process of Bible Study:* The best Bible Studies use the inductive process with its three steps: Observation (What does the passage say?), Interpretation (What was the author's intended meaning?), and Application (How does this apply to me today?). This is the best way to study the Bible. Look what's there. Figure out what it means and teaches you. Then, make an application to your life.

- *Are there associated podcasts or videos?* If they are to access these before you meet, tell them how to listen to the podcasts or find the videos to watch. Otherwise,

- *Are there Old Testament or New Testament summaries?* Reading any short Old Testament or New Testament summaries in the introduction is helpful if you have new members to your group and if you have anyone who is new to the Bible. You are helping them get started. Otherwise, you can recommend the women read them at home.

- *Go over the "Discussion Group Guidelines" for your group.* You can use the suggested ones in the study guide or add your own. It is good to have some guidelines for any group— whether you know each other well or if you have a lot of new members. Guidelines put everyone on a level relationship.

- *Is there any explanation about the theme of the study?* Sometimes, this is covered in an introductory podcast or video. If not, read any theme explanations together. This will help to generate interest in the study. This will cast a vision for them and generate interest in making this study a priority in their lives.

I like to know where I am going on a journey. I bet you do too. It is like having a tour brochure giving you the highlights of the tour. So read any parts of the Introduction that will benefit your group.

Walk through the first lesson

Have them open their study guides to the first lesson. Show them what to expect as they begin their study at home. This is valuable even if you plan to work through the study together each time you meet.

- *Cover the ABCs—Author, Background and Context.* This generally applies to Bible studies that cover a specific book of the Bible. A is for the author(s) of that book of the Bible. B is for the background of the time period in which it was written. C is for context, how the book fits into the rest of the Bible— Old Testament, New Testament, history, poetry, prophecy, gospels, letters of Paul, etc.

Bible studies that cover a specific book of the Bible should include information about this. But if not, you can find this information in good commentaries and online websites. Like the summaries and theme explanation, this gives the group members a solid footing to answer their Bible Study questions and make them hungry to learn more. So make this as interesting as you can.

- *Look at how the lesson is arranged.* Point out any different parts of the lesson. Is it divided into daily study sections? Some are and some aren't. Are there any extra research questions? How are the application questions identified? Is there a personal study section and a "listen to teaching" section? Is there a place to journal your faith story related to the lesson? Point out the different parts of the lesson as needed.

- *Begin to do the lesson together if you have time.* This demonstrates to anyone new to Bible Study how to work through questions by reading the verses and answering the question. If you get through part of the lesson, ask them to finish the rest of it at home. Otherwise, remind them to work on all of Lesson One at home before you get together again the next time.

- *Offer to help anyone new to the Bible.* Tell those new to Bible Study that if they have any questions about the lesson to contact you. If you have several new women and several experienced at Bible studies, consider asking the experienced ones to partner with the new ones during the week, getting together to work the lesson.

- *Encourage them to discover God's Word on their own during the week and make time to complete the lesson.* That way they can share with each other what they have learned. But come to the group even if they cannot complete the lesson. They will learn from the others.

See you are already guarding content.

Collect prayer requests and pray:

Ask the Lord Jesus to teach you what He wants you all to learn through this study. Commit your time and your personal Bible Study time to Him. Say yes to this adventure together.

Optional: Finish with a worship song.

I usually find one on YouTube that is addressed to the Lord and is easy to sing as a group. Show it on the TV screen where you meet, or print out the words and just play the song from your phone or tablet.

RECAP

In this chapter, you learned the value of making a positive first impression, ways to introduce the study to generate interest, and how to help your group get started on the lessons.

In Chapter 5, we will cover how to plan your group discussion for each lesson.

USE THE "FIRST DAY OF BIBLE STUDY" CHECKLIST ON THE NEXT PAGE TO HELP
YOU PREPARE FOR THE FIRST DAY YOU MEET WITH YOUR GROUP.

"First Day of Bible Study" checklist

Permission is granted to make copies of this checklist as needed.

Start with prayer

Pray for your group members that their hearts and minds would be open to whatever Jesus wants to teach them through the study and to learn how to love one another well.

Make a positive first impression as "Community Builder"

- ✓ Make sure that everyone can see and hear you and, if possible, see each other. Make adjustments to chairs and tables and where you sit to make this happen.

- ✓ Sit so that you face the entrance to the room. If someone comes late, you can quickly give a welcome smile and even a wave to let them know you are happy to see them.

- ✓ Introduce yourself and start with 1-2 general "get acquainted" questions, something that all the members have in common.

Confirm communication details and schedule.

- ✓ Best way to communicate with each one: Text, email, Facebook, phone call. Get their contact information if you do not have it, and give them permission to contact you if they do not understand what a question is asking

- ✓ Schedule and start time: It is a good idea to give them a schedule so they will know what lesson will be discussed on which date. Tell them when you will start and stop the group discussion so they will know.

- ✓ Sharing prayer requests: Talk about how you will share prayer requests—in the large group, small groups, or emailed to group members. Tell them what to do about "Private" requests.

Confirm all have Bibles and study guides.

- ✓ Make sure everyone has a Bible or Bible app (suggest a good one that is easy to use).

- ✓ Ask if anyone is new to studying the Bible. Make a note to yourself that that person might need help learning how to find Bible verses and answer questions.

- ✓ Make sure everyone has a Bible Study book or knows where to get one.

- ✓ Find out who is not comfortable reading aloud and remember not to call on her to read a Bible verse or paragraph in the book.

Introduce the study as the "CONTENT GUARDIAN"

- ✓ Look at the "Contents" page to generate interest in the study. Lesson titles often give clues as to what they will learn in that lesson.

- ✓ Will you do one lesson per group time or take two sessions to do one lesson?

Scan the "Introduction" section.

- ✓ Talk about the process of Bible Study: Observation (What does the passage say?), Interpretation (What was the author's intended meaning?), and Application (How does this apply to me today?).

- ✓ Tell how to listen to associated podcasts or find the videos to watch.

- ✓ Are there Old Testament or New Testament summaries? Read other pertinent information and explanation of the theme of the study. Or recommend the women read them at home.

- ✓ Go over the "Discussion Group Guidelines" for your group. You can use the suggested ones in the study guide or add your own. Guidelines put everyone on a level relationship.

Walk through the first lesson

- ✓ Cover the ABCs—Author, Background and Context. This generally applies to Bible studies that cover a specific book of the Bible.

- ✓ Look at how the lesson is arranged. Is it divided into daily study sections? Are there any extra research questions? How are the application questions identified? Is there a personal study section and a "listen to teaching" section?.

- ✓ Begin to do the lesson together if you have time or remind them to work on all of Lesson One at home before you get together again the next time.

- ✓ *Offer to help anyone new to the Bible.* Ask experienced ones to partner with the new ones during the week, getting together to work the lesson.

Collect prayer requests and pray:

- ✓ Ask the Lord Jesus to teach you what He wants you all to learn through this study. Commit your time and your personal Bible Study time to Him. Say yes to this adventure together.

Optional: Finish with a worship song.

Chapter 5: Prepare Wisely as Content Guardian

We are on this adventure together learning how to lead a Bible Study group with confidence and grace. The last chapter included making a positive first impression and introducing the study to get the group members excited about it. Yes!

Remember the two roles of a Bible Study group leader:

- *Role #1: Content Guardian*—guarding how the truth from God's Word is presented and received. As Content Guardian for your group, you have authority to control the content of the Bible Study discussion.

- *Role #2: Community Builder*—built around shared study and application of God's Word. As Community Builder for your group, you manage the group interaction to help them love one another well.

Doing these roles effectively leads to a healthy group.

In this chapter, we will focus on your role as the **Content Guardian** for your group. The Content Guardian maintains control of the truth from God's Word and makes sure it is handled correctly. As the one who is going to lead the discussion of the Bible verses, you have that authority under Jesus. So you need to know how to prepare wisely as the content guardian.

If you feel inadequate to lead a Bible Study, everyone feels that way when they are just starting out leading a study. You are not alone in how you feel. Who makes you able to lead a Bible Study? Jesus does! It is okay to feel a bit scared. When you are scared, you will rely on His power more. He will give you the confidence and grace to keep going.

It is okay to say, "Lord, I'm nervous. I feel like I don't know enough. I know I can't do this alone. I will trust you to do this in me and through me." Watch what He does!

WORK THROUGH THE LESSON YOURSELF

Always start with prayer!

Ask Jesus to help you learn what He wants you to know from the lesson and show you how to lead the discussion. Depend on Him to guide you through the Holy Spirit living inside you.

Be a learner before being a teacher.

Expect to learn something new or that enhances what you already know. This is what the Bible says about itself:

> For the word of God is **alive** and **active**. Sharper than any double-edged sword, it penetrates even to dividing soul and spirit, joints and marrow; it judges the thoughts and attitudes of the heart. (Hebrews 4:12)

God's Word is alive and active. No matter how many times I have read a particular passage of the Bible, something new almost always jumps out at me when I am studying it again. Expect to learn something new or better.

Enhance the study with what the Word teaches you.

As you open yourself to the Holy Spirit's leading, what you learn in your personal study time will be valuable to your group as you lead them through the discussion. A published Bible Study with questions for you to answer is just a guide.

As you do the study, you may think of follow-up questions to ask your group. Or you may consider a different way of asking a confusing question.

Yet, try to stay focused on the Bible passage you are studying rather than following rabbit trails. Your group will appreciate that.

Respond to the Spirit's prompting regarding the verses you are studying.

Stay true to what the Bible actually says.

You want to avoid the "look-imagine-see" way of looking at any verse. What does that look like? You *look* at the passage, *imagine* a way for it to fit a particular cultural slant, then you *see* what you want to see.

Cultural influence on Bible Study feeds this "look-imagine-see" process. It is very dangerous. Avoid doing that yourself. And be on guard for this with your group. That is why the "Observation" step in the inductive process of Bible Study is so important.

Use reliable study tools as needed.

Use good study aids to increase understanding, such as these:

- Bible.org—It is one of the largest Bible resource websites in the world where you can get quality biblical research and commentary on any topic or passage.

- soniclight.com—Access Dr. Tom Constable's Study Notes (verse by verse commentary on every book of the Bible, free to download or read online).

- blueletterbible.org—Use for translation comparisons and original Hebrew and Greek word meanings (called "Interlinear"). This is also available as the blueletterbible app for your phone or tablet.

- Gotquestions.org—Prepared answers to the most common questions about the Bible.

Of course, there are many study Bibles and commentaries available in book form as well.

MAKE A PLAN FOR LEADING THE LESSON

After you finished working through the lesson for yourself, the next step is to review the lesson to make your plan for leading the discussion.

Remember this as you do so. As Content Guardian, one of your goals is to help others learn to feed themselves too.

Start with prayer!

Like everything else you have learned so far, the best place to start is asking Jesus to help you make a plan. It is okay to make a plan. Just hand it to Him and give Him permission to change it.

As He guides you through the Holy Spirit's leading, what you learn in your personal study time will be valuable to your group as you lead them through the discussion.

Jesus will show you what the overall focus of your group discussion time should be, especially as you get to know the group members better.

Remember, it is good to say, "Lord Jesus, I can't do this on my own. I will trust you to do this through me."

As you prepare to lead, consider how you will be humble and gracious in your leadership. Jesus is our best example. He demonstrated for us that you can maintain truth in a group setting while still being humble and gracious in the process. He will help you do that too. Then, watch what He does!

Three options for types of studies

You can identify three main categories of Bible Studies for which you will plan discussion.

Option 1: Bible Study guides without videos

Option 2: Bible Study guides with video teaching

Option 3: Bible Study without using a published guide.

Through the years, I have used various ways to write a plan for leading a lesson—scrap paper, lots of sticky notes or flags, etc. Now, I find it easiest to just use colored pencils to mark the questions I'll cover and the Bible passages / paragraphs we will read aloud. I cross out the questions, the Bible verses, and paragraphs we will skip. I write extra questions or notes in the margins and draw an arrow to where it fits in the lesson.

Practice speaking through your plan.

You might not need to do this, but I practice speaking through my discussion plan even after all these years. If you get nervous speaking in front of people, read the questions aloud and consider how you will ask someone to read the Bible verses. You can also practice how you will cover the application questions and respond to potential rabbit trails or challenging questions.

Whether you have 45 minutes or 2 hours, it is okay to stay focused on what you decide is best, under Jesus' guidance, of course. All of this is part of preparing wisely as the Content Guardian of your group.

On the following pages, we will look at each of the three options of planning Bible Studies to lead for your group. Preparation for leading each is slightly different. But you will see that all of them have several things in common:

✓ Start with prayer: Ask Jesus to teach you what He wants you to learn from the lesson.

✓ Review the lesson to plan how to lead it—what to cover, what to skip, what to add

✓ Select the main Bible passages to read in group time that are the focus of the lesson

✓ End with prayer: Ask Jesus to apply in your lives what you learned through His Word.

Happy planning!

FIND THE CHECKLIST FOR EACH OPTION IN THE RESOURCES SECTION AT THE
END OF THIS BOOK.

OPTION 1: PLAN THE DISCUSSION FOR STUDY GUIDES WITHOUT VIDEOS

The following suggestions are based on the structure of most *Joyful Walk Bible Studies.*

Start with prayer: Ask Jesus to help you make a plan. He knows you and the women in your group well. He will guide you as you plan how to lead a lesson.

Review the lesson to plan how you will lead it: If you have a tendency to forget details, make notes directly in the study book next to each question to remind yourself what you want to do (colored pencils, sticky notes, margins).

> Remember this: You are the Content Guardian for the group and have the authority to determine what your group will cover.

Plan how and when you will start at the time you said you would start:

- Use an icebreaker or reporting back on last week's prayer requests.

- Ask what grabbed their attention in the lesson to let you know what interests them.

- Or start with prayer and the first question. Always start with prayer before you begin the discussion, asking Jesus to teach you what He wants you to learn from the lesson.

Determine how much of the lesson to cover based on your group meeting time.

- If you have a couple of hours, you can usually cover the whole lesson with time for creative discussion of any application questions.

- If you have only an hour or less, you can pre-select the questions you will cover and let the group members know ahead of time. This can help prevent some from being disappointed when their favorite question isn't being discussed. This works for busy people too. It also prevents feeling rushed trying to get through all of them. That is not good.

- You can also do this for a group where everyone is new to the Bible. Choose which questions they should do and which they should skip just to get started learning how to do Bible Study.

- If skipping questions bothers you, I mentioned earlier the option of dividing the lesson into two sessions. Regardless of how much time you have, stay focused on what you decide is best for the group. Remember you are the Content Guardian.

Always read the main Bible passages that are the focus of the lesson.

- Guide your group into the living, transforming Word of God by opening and reading the Bible together. Wise preparation plans to read the important Bible verses for the lesson. Mark the ones you will read in the group.

- If you skip reading the Bible passages, and just discuss the questions, then you will be spending your group time on "man's" word or "woman's" word rather than on God's revealed Word and your response to that.

- Also, don't assume that everyone has already read the Bible passages before coming to the group. It is better to skip questions and read the Bible passages than the other way around.

Mark the questions you will cover as well as those that can be combined or skipped without affecting the discussion.

- *Mark the questions you will cover as written.* Put a check mark on those you will cover as written. Don't just pick the application questions, thinking they are the most important. Pick questions related to the Bible passages being covered so you can make sure your group members understand the truth revealed in the Bible before they try to apply it in their lives.

- *Mark any extra questions you add from your own study.* I usually write these in the margin of my book and draw a circle around them to catch my eye.

- *Mark any questions that could be combined together into one general discussion.* Combine questions on a similar topic by asking, "What did you learn about…?" Some published Bible Studies have a small group discussion guide in the back of the book. These may have some questions already combined for you. Consider using those.

- *Mark any questions that could be skipped without affecting the discussion.* It's okay to skip some questions. Try not to skip too many observation questions, though. These are the most important part of Bible Study—learning to see what is actually in the text. You want to make sure the group members are basing their answers on what is in God's Word, not something they have heard before and not something they are imagining to be there. You want to avoid that "look-imagine-see" way of looking at the Bible.

- *Mark anything that might be confusing.* For the confusing questions, give your group permission to contact you through the week if they don't understand what a question is asking. Or let them know about a question ahead of time if you've seen it. Consider another way of asking the question.

- *Mark anything that might lead to extra discussion not related to the lesson.* Good discussion should stimulate additional questions and comments. People like to follow "rabbit trails." As the Content Guardian, you have to keep the group focused on what they need to learn from the lesson. Write yourself a "Watch out for this" note in the margin of the lesson. Some studies have extra research questions that you may not have time to cover in your meeting. But you might include good follow-up questions from your own study that will help the discussion and the learning process.

- *If you tend to be talkative, mark the question(s) where you want to share an answer.* Otherwise, let the group members answer the questions.

- *Decide how to cover the application questions:* In *Joyful Walk Bible Studies,* the application questions are easily identified by a focus phrase after the question number. Some questions are better for the whole group to discuss together. Some questions are too personal so they should be skipped, or they might not be relevant for your group. Some applications are great for smaller groups of 2-4 people turning their chairs together. I call this "Table Talk" whether you have tables or not and use this especially when I am leading a group bigger than 8. Give them a 3-5 minutes and use a timer.

  Let me add a caution here: Don't break up into smaller groups unless you know the group members well enough to be confident in the kind of biblical advice they might be sharing. It is better to stay in a larger group than to have to undo some bad teaching shared in a smaller group. I often ask someone I know and whose biblical understanding I can trust to be the leader for my smaller Table Talk groups.

End on time and with prayer: Be faithful to end at the time designated for your group. Ask the Lord Jesus to apply in your lives what you learned through His Word.

FIND THE CHECKLIST FOR OPTION 1 IN THE RESOURCES SECTION AT THE END OF THIS BOOK.

OPTION 2: PLAN THE DISCUSSION FOR STUDY GUIDES WITH VIDEO TEACHING

The following is based on my experience with study guides published by Lifeway.

Start with prayer: Ask Jesus to help you make a plan. He knows you and the women in your group well. He will guide you as you plan how to lead a lesson.

Review the lesson to plan how you will lead it: If you have a tendency to forget details, make notes directly in the study book next to each question to remind yourself what you want to do.

Remember this: You are the Content Guardian for the group and have the authority to determine what your group will cover.

Plan how and when you will start at the time you said you would start:

- Use an icebreaker or reporting back on last week's prayer requests.

- Ask what grabbed their attention in the lesson to let you know what interests them.

- Or start with prayer and the first question. Always start with prayer before you begin the discussion, asking Jesus to teach you what He wants you to learn from the lesson.

Determine how much of the lesson to cover based on your group meeting time.

- When dealing with the long lessons of most video-driven studies, you have to be selective in what you include in your group discussion. Usually, any group discussion time is an hour or less. Let your group know that you will be pre-selecting which questions and commentary to cover in your discussion time.

- This is good for a group where everyone is new to the Bible. Choose which questions they should do and which they should skip just to get started learning how to do Bible Study.

- If you will watch the video together, find out how long it is to determine how much time you have for discussing the Bible Study part.

- If skipping questions bothers you, I mentioned earlier the option of dividing the lesson into two sessions. Regardless of how much time you have, stay focused on what you decide is best for the group. Remember you are the Content Guardian.

Always read the main Bible passages that are the focus of the lesson.

- Guide your group into the living, transforming Word of God by opening and reading the Bible together. Wise preparation plans to read the important Bible verses for the lesson. Mark the ones you will read in the group.

- If you skip reading the Bible passages, and just discuss the questions, then you will be spending your group time on "man's" word or "woman's" word rather than on God's revealed Word and your response to that.

- Don't assume that everyone has already read the Bible passages before coming to the group. It is better to skip questions and read the Bible passages than the other way around.

Plan to watch or discuss the video teaching AFTER you have looked at the Bible verses and discussed the lesson.

- You want to talk more about God's Word than the author's or speaker's words. You should do the Bible Study first, even if the discussion guide recommends watching the video first.

Select the main Bible passages and associated questions / paragraphs from each day's study that you will cover. Give yourself permission to skip the rest.

- *Mark the main Bible passages and associated questions from each day's study.* Most video-driven studies are divided into five days of individual study. Choose what you consider to be most important for discussing. Don't just pick the application questions, thinking they are the most important. Pick questions related to the Bible passages being covered so you can make sure your group members understand the truth revealed in the Bible before they try to apply it in their lives.

- *Choose explanatory paragraphs that are helpful to understand the Bible passages.* Mark these in your study guide so you can recognize them easily as you lead—colored pencils, marginal notes, dog-eared pages, sticky flags, whatever works.

- *Mark anything that might be confusing.* For the confusing questions, give your group permission to contact you through the week if they don't understand what a question is asking. Or let them know about a question ahead of time if you've seen it. Consider another way of asking the question if it is an important one or a good follow-up question from your own study.

- *Mark anything that might lead to extra discussion not related to the lesson.* Good discussion should stimulate additional questions and comments. People like to follow "rabbit trails." As the Content Guardian, you have to keep the group focused on what they need to learn from the lesson. Write yourself a "Watch out for this" note in the margin of the lesson..

- *If you tend to be talkative, mark the question(s) where you want to share an answer.* Otherwise, let the group members answer the questions.

Scan the suggested discussion guide questions for anything valuable to use.

- In most video-driven studies, there are discussion questions for the lesson and separate ones for the video. The suggested guides often contain mostly application questions and "how do you feel about…" or "do you think…" questions. A few of these are okay. But focusing on your feelings and opinions are not good for guiding your group into God's Word. Emotional responses should follow understanding God's truth and how it applies to you. That is why you should always do your Bible Study first before watching any video teaching.

Choose how to cover the application questions:

- Some application questions are better for the whole group to discuss together. Some questions are too personal so they should be skipped, or they might not be relevant for your group. Some applications are great for smaller groups of 2-4 people turning their chairs together. I call this "Table Talk" whether you have tables or not and use this especially when I am leading a group bigger than 8. Give them a 3-5 minutes and use a timer.

  Let me add a caution here: Don't break up into smaller groups unless you know the group members well enough to be confident in the kind of biblical advice they might be sharing. It is better to stay in a larger group than to have to undo some bad teaching shared in a smaller group. I often ask someone I know and whose biblical understanding I can trust to be the leader for my smaller Table Talk groups.

End on time and with prayer: Be faithful to end at the time designated for your group. Ask the Lord Jesus to apply in your lives what you learned through His Word.

FIND THE CHECKLIST FOR OPTION 2 IN THE RESOURCES SECTION AT THE END OF THIS BOOK.

OPTION 3: PLAN THE DISCUSSION FOR BIBLE STUDY WITHOUT A STUDY GUIDE

If you are an experienced Bible Study leader, you can certainly lead a Bible Study group through a book of the Bible without using a published study guide.

PREPARATION OF THE STUDY

Start with prayer:

Ask the Lord Jesus to lead you to the book of the Bible your group should study. We recommend starting in the New Testament with Mark or Philippians. Ask the Lord Jesus to teach you through His word.

Research the ABC's of the book you will be studying:

Gather information on the Author, the Background setting for the story (historical setting, why it was written), and the Context (where the book fits into the Bible).

Divide up the book into passages you will cover in each lesson.

This will depend upon the number of times your group will meet. Give a schedule to your group members so they will know what passage to read and study on their own each week. Suggest they choose one verse from that passage to dwell upon all week long and ask God to teach them through that verse.

Follow the Inductive process in your study and as you lead the lesson discussion:

Observation (What does the passage say?), Interpretation (What was the author's intended meaning?), and Application (How does this apply to me today?). Teach your group how to use this method in their preparation. Show them how to use online study tools. See what is listed in Chapter 5.

Look up words you do not understand in a dictionary or Bible dictionary.

Consider asking these questions as you observe each passage:

What grabbed your attention from these verses? That will help you gauge what interested them.

What verses or specific words do you want to understand better?

What words or phrases are repeated in this passage?

What topics (if any) in this passage have we studied in previous lessons?

Which verse did you choose to dwell upon and why?

Consider applications from what you learned:

Consider how you can lead your group members to apply what they learn.

PLANNING TO LEAD EACH LESSON

Start with prayer: Ask Jesus to help you make a plan. He knows you and the women in your group well. He will guide you as you plan how to lead a lesson.

Review the lesson to plan how you will lead it: If you have a tendency to forget details, make notes to remind yourself what you want to do. This would be based on your preparation for the story and what you want to cover each week.

Remember this: You are the Content Guardian for the group and have the authority to determine what your group will cover.

Plan how and when you will start at the time you said you would start:

- Use an icebreaker or reporting back on last week's prayer requests.

- Ask what grabbed their attention in the lesson to let you know what interests them.

- Or start with prayer and begin reading the passage. Always start with prayer before you begin the discussion, asking Jesus to teach you what He wants you to learn from the lesson.

Always read the main Bible passage that is the focus of the lesson.

- Guide your group into the living, transforming Word of God by opening and reading the Bible together. Wise preparation plans to read the important Bible verses for the lesson. Mark the ones you will read in the group.

- If you skip reading the Bible passages, and just discuss your planned questions, then you will be spending your group time on "man's" word or "woman's" word rather than on God's revealed Word and your response to that.

- Also, don't assume that everyone has already read the Bible passages before coming to the group. It is better to skip some questions and read the Bible passages than the other way around.

Work through the verses in context by paragraphs.

- Ask what grabbed their attention from initial reading.

- Ask questions about what the text says. What is happening? What were people thinking and feeling? What truth is presented that corrects specific error in thinking?

- Look up and/or discuss meanings of words that are relevant.

- Stay Christ-focused, emphasizing what He is saying to you through His Word and how you can obey Him and depend upon Him more in your life.

- Consider how you can apply what you learned.

Choose how to cover the application questions

- Some application questions are better for the whole group to discuss together. Some questions are too personal so they should be skipped, or they might not be relevant for your group. Some applications are great for smaller groups of 2-4 people turning their chairs together. I call this "Table Talk" whether you have tables or not and use this especially when I am leading a group bigger than 8. Give them a 3-5 minutes and use a timer.

  Let me add a caution here: Don't break up into smaller groups unless you know the group members well enough to be confident in the kind of biblical advice they might be sharing. It is better to stay in a larger group than to have to undo some bad teaching shared in a smaller group. I often ask someone I know and whose biblical understanding I can trust to be the leader for my smaller Table Talk groups.

Limit your "teaching" time

- Consider how to keep the group members engaged in the study. That will involve an intentional act on your part to resist a lot of "teaching," especially since you have done so much work preparing the study. The goal is for them to learn from the Bible for themselves and not depend on you.

- A wise experienced Bible teacher once shared with me that you can only share about 10% of what you have discovered in all your personal study time for a lecture or Bible Study lesson. I have found that to be especially true when it comes to historical, geographical, and biographical facts.

End on time and with prayer: Be faithful to end at the time designated for your group. Ask the Lord Jesus to apply in your lives what you learned through His Word.

FIND THE CHECKLIST FOR OPTION 3 IN THE RESOURCES SECTION AT THE END OF THIS BOOK.

RECAP

In this chapter, you learned how to prepare wisely by learning from the study for yourself first. Then, you learned how to prepare wisely by reviewing the lesson to make a simple plan. And you learned what a wise plan looks like.

In Chapter 6, we will look at how to lead a lesson graciously as the Content Guardian for your group.

Chapter 6: Lead Confidently as Content Guardian

So far you have learned how to choose a Bible Study for your group and how to make a positive first impression when you meet together. You have learned how to introduce the study so your group will be excited about learning together. And you have seen that you need to do the lesson for yourself first, feeding yourself from the Word of God. Then, you can review the lesson and make a simple plan to lead your group in wonderful Bible-focused, Christ-focused discussion.

Now we get to the part you have been anticipating. Leading the lesson confidently as the Content Guardian for your group.

GUIDELINES FOR THE CONTENT GUARDIAN

Guidelines are just good reminders of how to do something well. Some of these are restatements of what you learned in the previous chapters. Use these to humbly follow your plan.

#1. Start at your stated time.

Start at the time you said you would start with something—icebreaker, answered prayer, first question, what grabbed their attention in the lesson. This rewards those who come early and also encourages group members to plan on arriving on time.

#2. Guide your group into reading the Bible together.

Remind the women and yourself that this is a Bible Study. It is not a "read his or her words and discuss" activity. You want them to discover God's Word for themselves. It is the living, transforming Word of God.

#3. Encourage everyone to learn from the lesson on their own.

You want them to discover treasures from God's Word during the week, taking time to complete the lesson, and then to share with each other what they have learned.

Sometimes I will read a question then say, *"What did you learn from this as you did your lesson?"* This reinforces that they would learn more from doing their lessons before coming to the group.

#4. Read the question and wait for the group to respond.

Let them share what they have discovered. Don't jump in and answer a question. Wait for them to respond. Silence is okay! Count to 10 before jumping in! Let them have time to think. Repeat the question if no one answers. It is best to let them respond at will.

If one person can't stand the silence and keeps jumping in, use humor and grace to ask others to join in the discussion. You can say, *"We can't let her answer all the questions, can we?"*

56. Move on after someone gives an answer for those questions requiring one answer.

This is one way to keep moving through the lesson. Usually those are observation questions.

#6. Ask, "Anyone else?" for those questions requiring several answers until the ones you think are important have been shared.

Have in mind which questions require more answers. You want to get all, not just a piece. Give them time to consider more answers.

#7. Be ready if a question causes someone to get emotional.

Put an arm around her, affirm her hurt, and pray for her. Then say, "Let's see how we can learn to trust God even in the midst of our hurt." Move on.

#8. Communicate acceptance in your eyes, manner, and response to what is shared.

They need to trust that you won't make quick judgments about them. You might need to practice your facial expressions as you wait for answers and listen to them. Try to be unshockable. Not always possible. At least try.

#9. Affirm those who share, especially if they are normally quiet.

Say, "Thank you for sharing that." Say her name so others will know it as well because she is usually quiet.

#10. Clarify the truth gently if the comment needs further explanation.

Correct error gently if it is important to the discussion. Especially if what was said is not in the Bible text. I try to always point them back to what the Scripture actually says. You want them to see what is there not what they want it to say.

#11. Limit your own talking except to lead the discussion and to direct it or enhance it with something amazing that you learned.

We learn so much on our own as we prepare to lead a lesson. But share your answers when necessary or if something totally amazed you. It is okay to show you are a learner too. Mark those you will share.

#12. Avoid getting bogged down on any one issue.

This is where you pay attention to any notes you made about possible rabbit trails. Be aware of them. Stay focused on what you decide is best for the group. Keep the discussion moving along.

#13. Approach this role with humility and grace.

How do you do that? Be approachable and caring for your group. Let them know that you are learning right alongside them. Be excited about what they see in the Scriptures as they study. It always amazes me and humbles me to hear someone else discover something in the passage that I totally missed. Be that way too.

RECAP

In this chapter, you learned a few discussion leading guidelines that will benefit your group. These will encourage group members to participate in the discussion. Approach your role with humility and grace. This will help you lead confidently as the Content Guardian of your group

In Chapter 7, we will cover how to graciously handle some common challenges to leading a Bible Study.

Chapter 7: Lead Graciously as Community Builder

In this chapter, you will learn helpful suggestions to help you lead graciously as a Community Builder for your group.

Your two roles as a Bible Study leader are that of Content Guardian and Community Builder. They are linked together. How you manage the group discussion and the time together contributes to building community within the group.

Again, here is where you must depend on Jesus to help you with this. He knows the people in your group. He knows how He has gifted you and them. He can show you how to love them well.

THERE WILL BE CHALLENGES

You have done your studying of the lesson. You have asked Jesus to help you make a plan for leading it and given Him permission to change it as needed.

But even if you have the best plan for how to lead a lesson, there will be challenges to that plan because your group is made up of people.

All different kinds of people attend Bible Study groups—people who are unique, at different stages in their Christian growth, with a wide variety of experiences, and possessing different behavioral tendencies.

You will have a mixture of those who are shy, talkative, friendly, and standoffish. You might have some who like to argue or debate—whether from good motives or from a desire to be combative. You know what I am talking about.

Allow these words from Paul in Colossians 4 to give you guidance,

> *Let your conversation be always full of grace, seasoned with salt, so that you may know how to answer everyone. (Colossians 4:6)*

Let us consider what these phrases mean.

Conversation full of grace—

> Gracious speech. Grace is God's gift of kindness to us because He loves us. We can extend God's kindness to others in what we say. By faith.

Seasoned with salt—

> Tasty, inviting, making someone want more. We do this by faith as well.

That you may know how to answer anyone—

> This does not mean you must know all the answers. It does include thinking about how you will respond to what others say in various situations. We will cover this in the section below. Once again, you do this by faith.

Have you noticed how many times I have mentioned doing all of this by faith? The temptation is always to rely on your own experiences, knowledge, and preferences. Though you may have gained valuable skills for leading a group, only Jesus knows you, His Word, and the hearts of the women in your group.

In this chapter, we will look at a few of the common challenges that Bible Study leaders face—both experienced and new leaders. I will share with you some gracious, loving ways to respond to those challenges. Of course, this is not an exhaustive list. But we will use these common experiences to learn how to lead graciously as a community builder. **Trust in Jesus to help you do this**.

GRACIOUSLY RESPOND TO COMMON CHALLENGES

In this section, I'll help you learn how to graciously respond to common challenges that affect your leadership. I have identified several areas that have been challenges for me and might be challenges for you.

Challenge #1: Some are not doing their lessons ahead of time

- You cannot control this, so do not let it annoy you.

- Expect some to not have their lessons finished. Realize that some people are so busy with work, school, and family, that they have a hard time finding extra time to do another thing for themselves. It could be just the season of life. They want to be part of your group.

- Encourage them to come to the study anyway and learn as you read the Bible passages and discuss them together. Perhaps that will generate a desire to carve out time to do the lesson at home.

- Keep encouraging them to feed themselves from God's Word, even if they only do the first page of the lesson—to do something. But they should come to the study any way and learn as you read the Bible passages and discuss them together.

- If this is the majority of your group, pick a shorter Bible Study that can be done in one sitting. Make it easier for them to be successful.

Challenge #2: Encouraging everyone to participate in the discussion.

- It is not your job to make everyone talk. I have been told by the shy and quiet people that they prefer to listen. If they have something to say, they will say it. You don't have to force opportunity for them to talk. Be sure to affirm their answers when they do!

- You can always ask the quiet ones if they need encouragement to talk in the large group. It is not your job to make them do that.

- You can offer small groups of 2-4 people to discuss some questions such as application questions. This helps the quieter ones feel the freedom to share. But remember, only do this if you can trust what the women will share with one another.

- Avoid calling on people to make them participate. They might not come back. Use the "Whoever wants to go next" method. You will build community more effectively if you let people respond when they feel ready to do so.

- Limit your own talking except to lead the discussion once it begins. Share your answers when necessary or if something totally amazed you.

- As you lead, listen well and affirm answers. This encourages participation as they feel comfortable.

Challenge #3: Managing the talkative and argumentative people graciously.

Your goal is not to allow them to dominate the discussion, right?

Talkative:

- When someone gets really long in their answer, ask Jesus to help you think of words you can use to jump in and sum up what they just said. Use humor. Quickly thank them for an answer, turn your eyes away, and move on. You can also ask Jesus to have another person in the group jump into the discussion graciously. Keep being gracious about this. Firm but gracious.

- If you have people who know they talk too much in your group, talk with them outside of class and let them know that you would like them to keep their answers shorter. Work out a signal between the two of you when she is talking too much. If you do it graciously, most people will respond just fine.

- If you are the talkative one my friend, mark the question(s) where you will share an answer. Otherwise, let the rest of the group members answer the questions.

Argumentative:

- If you have someone who likes to argue with you, ask a couple of women in the group to pray with you beforehand and sit on each side of you during the class session. While you are leading, ask them to pray silently if they feel any discord or if they sense the individual being problematic in any way. Try to answer the relevant questions being asked, but then offer to meet the individual following the study to answer any other questions that she might have. See my handbook, *Be a Christ-Focused Small Group Leader*, for more ideas about dealing with argumentative people.

Remember you are the Content Guardian. The group depends on you to not let a talkative or argumentative person take control of your group.

Challenge #4: The temptation to "fix" each other's problems

- When people in your group start opening up about the issues they have and challenges they face, it is so tempting to group members to want to jump in and "fix it" for them. Don't let this happen. That is not good for community building.

- It is not the group's job to fix each other. That belongs to Jesus.

- Tell them up front, "We are not going to try to fix each other's issues. We will be good listeners." As the leader, point everyone to depend on Jesus to show them a way out of any challenge.

- If you have "Table Talk" time with smaller groups, say to them, "When you share your own lives and how Jesus has helped you, the others in your group will hear that. If they want to ask you questions about it, get together with them later."

- You will have to keep reminding them and yourself not to jump in and "fix it." Interrupt it whenever it happens.

Challenge #5: Fear of not knowing the answers

- Assume you will get asked questions for which you do not know the answers. That is a given! And it's okay. You are not expected to have all the answers. No one does!

- Stay focused on the lesson. Dwell on what you can know. It's okay to focus on what you do know and what you want the group to be confident in knowing related to the lesson.

- Avoid speculation just to come up with an answer. Humbly accept what you cannot know or do not understand.

- Don't fret about not being able to answer someone's question. Assume it will happen and graciously say, "I don't know." If it's important enough, try to find out. You can even challenge her to look up the answer.

- Give your group the same online resources that I gave you in Chapter 3. Gotquestions.org is a great source for answers to many questions about the Bible.

Challenge #6: Choosing a Bible Study that everyone likes

- This is not likely to happen. Don't even open it up to the group for a choice. Maybe, you can share your ideas with a co-leader or friend.

- Pray about what is best for the group.

- Choose what interests you and where you would like to grow in your faith. If you are passionate about what you are studying, that will be infectious to the rest of the group.

- Remind them that group Bible Study is about "we" and not all about "me." It is about the whole group learning together.

- For those who might have already studied that book of the Bible you chose, suggest to them that this might be the time when they help someone else understand it. The Word of God is alive and active. If she is open to it, she will learn something new.

- If someone who has been in Bible Studies for years complains that the study you chose is too easy, ask them to be mentors to others who are new to Bible Study.

- This is a great time for them to invite a friend or co-worker who is new to the Bible to attend this one. Then, they can come alongside the new person as a mentor.

- Go ahead, you choose the study and be excited about it.

Challenge #7: Feeling overwhelmed with the responsibility

- Overseeing a Bible Study group may seem like a lot of work. But I have some suggestions to help you overcome that feeling.

- When your group is put together, invite someone in the group to help you with some of the responsibility of the group: administration, communicating with the women, or room setup. It is always good to have someone else take ownership of the group besides you. It helps you to not feel overwhelmed, and it gives experience to someone else in leading a group.

- Ask a trustworthy person in your group to be willing and prepared to step in and lead the lesson if something happens to you one day. You can give her your plan or suggest she make her own.

- If you already have a coleader, the two of you could share lesson leading and follow-up with the women between meeting times. Gaining experience in establishing others in their faith is part of Jesus' commission to us for disciplemaking.

- Another thing you can do is to ask outgoing women to help you make others feel connected to the group. This helps them use their natural gifts. And it is good for the group.

- So don't let a feeling of responsibility for the group overwhelm you. If Jesus gave you this desire to lead a group, He is the one who makes you able. You can't do it on your own anyway. At least, not well. Trust Him for someone to help you.

Challenge #8: Getting nervous speaking in front of people

- If you get really nervous about leading a study regardless of how much time you have put in to study the lesson and prepare your plan, here are my suggestions:

- Practice speaking through your plan: asking questions, asking someone to read the Bible verses, and explaining how you will do the application questions if you choose to do any in smaller groups. I do all of that still, after all these years.

- Put reminder notes in strategic places in the lesson where your memory needs some help. I do this too.

- Consider how you'll respond to potential rabbit trails or challenging questions. Do this with a smile. Remember to not act shocked.

- Practice helps. Saying things out loud helps us to remember it better and to work out any awkward phrasing. Anything worth doing well is worth practicing.

Challenge #9: When group members are not connecting with the group

- Recognize who is not connecting with the group. If you have newcomers to your group, or those who do not already feel connected, make an effort to connect with them personally. Be proactive about this.

- When you intentionally connect with someone who is on the "fringe" or the outside of the group, there is a higher likelihood that they will continue to try out the group.

- Be intentional about connecting her with the other group members. Pay attention to anything that person might have in common with others in the group. Some of your icebreaker questions can give that information as well as application questions. Connecting group members with each other benefits everyone in the group.

Challenge #10: When group members drop out

- Expect a few group members to drop out. Do not take it personally. You may be tempted to take it personally when people drop out of your group—whether they tell you they are dropping or they just stop coming.

- You might start wondering what you did wrong. Don't let this affect your confidence. Some people sign up for a Bible Study group with good intentions of doing the lessons and attending regularly. But life gets in the way. Give any feelings of insecurity to Jesus!

- It is okay to try to find out the reasons why they drop out. Do this without being defensive or suspicious. More than likely it is not your leadership but that person's season of life. Or their schedule has changed preventing them from continuing.

- You can ask a trusted friend to let you know if your leadership style might be pushing someone away. Like I have mentioned several times, be humble and gracious in your role as Content Guardian. If there is anything you can change to keep her coming, do that. Otherwise, just let it go.

OTHER CHALLENGES

List other challenges you have experienced or think you might experience in leading a Bible Study group. Consider how you would graciously respond to those challenges.

RECAP

You learned in this chapter how to graciously respond to common challenges you might experience while leading a Bible Stud group.

Ask Jesus to help you respond graciously to these challenges. Depend on Him to show you what to do. He is Faithful!

ADD YOUR IDEAS AND EXPERIENCES TO THE "COMMON CHALLENGES TO COMMUNITY BUILDING" WORKSHEET ON THE NEXT PAGE.

"Common Challenges to Community Building" worksheet

The following are some of the most common challenges that both experienced and new leaders face. Consider gracious, loving ways for you to respond to those challenges. Learn how to *Lead Graciously as a Community Builder*. Ask Jesus to help you with all of these challenges to leading a Bible Study group. Depend on Him to show you what to do. He is faithful!

Let your conversation be always full of grace, seasoned with salt, so that you may know how to answer everyone. (Colossians 4:6)

Challenge #1. Some are not doing their lessons ahead of time

You cannot control this, so do not let it annoy you. Realize that some people are so busy with work, school, and family, that they have a hard time finding extra time to do another thing for themselves. It could be just the season of life. Keep encouraging them to feed themselves from God's Word, even if they only do the first page of the lesson. But they should come to the study any way and learn as you read the Bible passages and discuss them together. If this is the majority of your group, pick a shorter Bible Study that can be done in one sitting.

Your ideas or experience:

Challenge #2. Encouraging everyone to participate in the discussion

It is not your job to make everyone talk. For those who are shy or quiet, try to offer small groups of 2-4 people to discuss some questions such as the application questions. Avoid calling on people to make them participate. Limit your own talking except to lead the discussion once it begins. Share your answers when necessary or if something totally amazed you. Listen well and affirm answers.

Your ideas or experience:

Challenge #3. Managing talkative and argumentative people graciously

Do not allow them to dominate the discussion. Ask Jesus to help you think of words you can use to jump in and sum up what they just said. Use humor. Quickly thank them for an answer, turn your eyes away, and move on. If you have people who know they talk too much in your group, work out a signal between the two of you when she is talking too much. Ask others to pray for you and the argumentative person as you lead the discussion. As the Content Guardian, the group depends on you to not let a talkative or argumentative person take control of your group. Ask Jesus to help you manage them graciously.

Your ideas or experience:

Challenge #4. The temptation to "fix" each other's problems

Don't let this happen. Interrupt this right away. It is not the group's job to fix each other. That belongs to Jesus. Tell them up front, "We are not going to try to fix each other's issues. We will be good listeners." As the leader, point everyone to depend on Jesus to show them a way out of any challenge. Tell them to listen to the others sharing their experiences. If they want to ask you questions about it, they can get together with them later.

Your ideas or experience:

Challenge #5. Fear of not knowing the answers

Assume this will happen. You won't know all the answers. Stay focused on the lesson. Dwell on what you can know from the lesson. Avoid speculation just to come up with an answer. Humbly accept what you cannot know or do not understand. Graciously say, "I don't know." If it's important enough, try to find out. Share good resources for that.

Your ideas or experience:

Challenge #6. Choosing a Bible Study that everyone likes

You will not be able to please everyone. Don't even open it up to the group for a choice. Pray about what is best for the group. If you are passionate about what you are studying, that will be infectious to the rest of the group. Communicate that group Bible Study is about "we" and not all about "me." If someone who has been in Bible Studies for years complains that the study you chose is too easy, ask them to be mentors to others who are new to Bible Study or have not already studied that topic. Choose the study and be excited about it.

Your ideas or experience:

Challenge #7. Feeling overwhelmed with the responsibility

Invite another group member to help you with some of the responsibility of the group: administration, communicating with the women, or leading the lesson. Let them take ownership of the group with you. Ask someone to be prepared to step in and lead the lesson if something happens to you one day. If you have a coleader, you could share lesson leading and follow-up with the women between meeting times. Trust Jesus for someone to help you so you won't feel overwhelmed.

Your ideas or experience:

Challenge #8. Getting nervous speaking in front of people

Practice speaking through your plan as you would in the group: asking questions, asking someone to read the Bible verses, and explaining how you will do the application questions if you choose to do any in smaller groups. Put reminder notes in strategic places in the lesson where your memory needs some help. Consider how you'll respond to potential rabbit trails or challenging questions. Saying things out loud helps us to remember it better and to work out any awkward phrasing.

Your ideas or experience:

Challenge #9. When group members are not connecting with the group

Recognize them. If you have newcomers to your group, or those who do not already feel connected, make an effort to connect with them personally. When you intentionally connect with someone who is on the "fringe" of the group, there is a higher likelihood that they will continue to try out the group. You will then have a better opportunity to connect her with the other group members. Be intentional about connecting her with the other group members by paying attention to anything that person might have in common with others in the group.

Your ideas or experience:

Challenge #10. When group members drop out

Do not take it personally. Give any feelings of insecurity to Jesus! Some sign up for a Bible Study group with good intentions of doing the lessons and attending regularly. But things get in the way. Try to find out the reasons why. More than likely it is not your leadership but that person's season of life. Or their schedule has changed preventing them from continuing. Ask a trusted friend to let you know if your leadership style might be pushing someone away. Like I have mentioned several times, be humble and gracious in your role as Content Guardian. If there is anything you can address with her or with the group to keep her coming, do that. Otherwise, just let it go.

Your ideas or experience:

May Jesus make your time as a Bible Study leader very fruitful for Him. Enjoy the blessings of discovering God's Word together with a group of people and watch each one experience a joyful walk with Jesus. It will be a great adventure!

Epilogue: Enjoy the Adventure

In this *Bible Study Leadership Made Easy* handbook, you have learned a lot as you have prepared to be a Content Guardian and Community Builder for your Bible Study group. You have come a long way!

Now, you are ready to enjoy the adventure as you step out in faith to lead a Bible Study next week, next month, or next year.

Remember that if you are still feeling inadequate to lead a Bible Study, everyone feels that way when they are just starting out. You are not alone in how you feel. And it is okay to feel a bit scared. Do you remember why? Who makes you able to lead a Bible Study? That's right. Jesus does!

Paul wrote about this in Colossians 1,

> *He is the one we proclaim, admonishing and teaching everyone with all wisdom, so that we may present everyone fully mature in Christ. To this end I strenuously contend with **all the energy Christ so powerfully works in me**. (Colossians 1:28-29)*

Rely on Jesus' power at work in you to give you the confidence and grace to keep going. Just say to Jesus, "Lord, I'm nervous. I feel like I don't know enough. I know I can't do this alone. I will trust you to do this in me and through me." Then, watch what He does!

May Jesus make your time as a Bible Study leader very fruitful for Him. Enjoy the blessings of discovering God's Word together with a group of people and watch each one experience a joyful walk with Jesus. It will be a great adventure!

WANT MORE HELP FOR LEADING A SMALL GROUP? KEEP READING TO SEE OUR RECOMMENDATIONS IN THE RESOURCES SECTION AT THE END OF THIS BOOK.

Option 1: Plan the Discussion for Study Guides without Videos

Permission is granted to make copies of this checklist as needed.

Start with prayer. Ask Jesus to help you make a plan. He knows you and the women in your group well. He will guide you as you plan how to lead a lesson.

Review the lesson to plan how you will lead it.

✓ If you have a tendency to forget details, make notes directly in the study book next to each question to remind yourself what you want to do. **You are the Content Guardian for the group and have the authority to determine what your group will cover.**

✓ *Start with something at the time you said you would start:* icebreaker, what jumped out at them in the lesson, or prayer and the first question.

✓ *Remember to pray before you begin the discussion.* Ask Jesus to teach you what He wants you to learn from the lesson.

✓ *Consider how long your group gets to meet to determine how much of the lesson to cover.* If you have a couple of hours, you can usually cover the whole lesson with time for creative discussion of any application questions. If you have only an hour or less, choose which questions you want to discuss as a group. Or split the lesson into two separate meeting times.

✓ *Always read the main Bible passages that are the focus of the lesson.* Mark those to read in the group. If you run short of time, skip questions but read the Bible verses.

✓ *Mark the questions you will cover as well as those that can be combined or skipped without affecting the discussion.* For anything that might be confusing or lead to extra discussion not related to the lesson (rabbit trails), write yourself a "Watch out for this" note in the margin of the study. Some studies have extra research questions that you may not have time to cover in your meeting. But you might include good follow-up questions from your own study that will help the discussion and the learning process.

✓ *If you tend to be talkative, mark the question(s)* where you want to share an answer. Otherwise, let the group members answer the questions.

✓ *Decide how to cover the application questions:* in large group, in small groups (2-4), or skipped (personal).

✓ *End on time and with prayer.* Be faithful to end at the time designated for your group. Ask the Lord Jesus to apply in your lives what you learned through His Word.

Practice speaking through your plan as needed.

✓ Read the questions aloud and how you will ask someone to read the Bible verses.

✓ Practice how you will cover the application questions and respond to potential rabbit trails or challenging questions.

Option 2: Plan the Discussion for Study Guides with Video Teaching

Permission is granted to make copies of this checklist as needed.

Start with prayer: Ask Jesus to help you make a plan. He knows you and the women in your group well. He will guide you as you plan how to lead a lesson.

Review the lesson to plan how you will lead it:

✓ *If you have a tendency to forget details,* make notes directly in the study book next to each question to remind yourself what you want to do. **You are the Content Guardian for the group and have the authority to determine what your group will cover**.

✓ *Start with something at the time you said you would start:* Icebreaker, what jumped out at them in the lesson, or prayer and the first question.

✓ *Remember to pray before you begin the discussion.* Ask Jesus to teach you what He wants you to learn from the lesson.

✓ *Consider how long your group gets to meet to determine how much of the lesson to cover.* Will you be covering the lesson in one or two sessions? If you will watch the video together, find out how long it is to determine how much time you have for discussing the Bible Study part.

✓ *Plan to watch or discuss the video teaching AFTER you have looked at the Bible verses and discussed the lesson.* You should do the Bible Study first, even if the discussion guide recommends watching the video first.

Select the main Bible passages and associated questions / paragraphs from each day's study that you will cover. Give yourself permission to skip the rest.

✓ *Mark the main Bible passages and associated questions from each day's study.* Pick questions related to the Bible passages being covered so you can make sure your group members understand the truth revealed in the Bible before they try to apply it in their lives with the application questions.

✓ *Choose explanatory paragraphs that are helpful to understand the Bible passages.* Mark these in your study guide so you can recognize them easily as you lead—colored pencils, marginal notes, dog-eared pages, sticky flags, whatever works.

✓ *Mark anything that might be confusing.* Give your group permission to contact you through the week if they don't understand what a question is asking. Or let them know about a question ahead of time if you've seen it. Consider another way of asking the question if it is an important one or a good follow-up question from your own study.

✓ *Mark anything that might lead to extra discussion not related to the lesson.* Good discussion should stimulate additional questions and comments. As the Content Guardian, you have to keep the group focused on what they need to learn from the lesson. Write yourself a "Watch out for this" note in the margin of the lesson..

✓ *If you tend to be talkative, mark the question(s) where you want to share an answer.* Otherwise, let the group members answer the questions.

Scan the suggested discussion guide questions for anything valuable to use.

✓ *Look at the discussion questions for the lesson.* Which ones will be usable for guiding your group into God's Word?

✓ *Look at the discussion questions for the video.* Which ones will be beneficial to your discussion of the lesson?

✓ *Decide how to cover the application questions:* in large group, in small groups (2-4), or skipped (personal).

✓ *End on time and with prayer.* Be faithful to end at the time designated for your group. Ask the Lord Jesus to apply in your lives what you learned through His Word.

Practice speaking through your plan as needed.

✓ Read the questions aloud and how you will ask someone to read the Bible verses.

✓ Practice how you will cover the application questions and respond to potential rabbit trails or challenging questions.

Option 3: Plan the Discussion for Bible Study without a Study Guide

Permission is granted to make copies of this checklist as needed.

PREPARATION OF THE STUDY

Start with prayer: Ask the Lord Jesus to lead you to the book of the Bible your group should study. We recommend starting in the New Testament with Mark or Philippians. Ask the Lord Jesus to teach you through His word.

Research the ABC's of the book you will be studying:

✓ Gather information on the Author, the Background setting for the story (historical setting, why it was written), and the Context (where the book fits into the Bible).

Divide up the book into passages you will cover in each lesson.

✓ Give a schedule to your group members so they will know what passage to read and study on their own each week. Suggest they choose one verse from that passage to dwell upon all week long and ask God to teach them through that verse.

Follow the Inductive process in your study and as you lead the lesson discussion:

✓ Observation (What does the passage say?), Interpretation (What was the author's intended meaning?), and Application (How does this apply to me today?). Teach your group how to use this method in their preparation.

✓ Show them how to use online study tools.

✓ Look up words you do not understand in a dictionary or Bible dictionary.

Consider asking these questions as you observe each passage:

- What grabbed your attention from these verses? That will help you gauge what interested them.

- What verses or specific words do you want to understand better?

- What words or phrases are repeated in this passage?

- What topics (if any) in this passage have we studied in previous lessons?

- Which verse did you choose to dwell upon and why?

Consider applications from what you learned:

✓ Consider how you can lead your group members to apply what they learn.

PLANNING TO LEAD EACH LESSON

Start with prayer: Ask Jesus to help you make a plan. He knows you and the women in your group well. He will guide you as you plan how to lead a lesson.

Review the lesson to plan how you will lead it:

✓ *If you have a tendency to forget details,* make notes directly in the study book next to each question to remind yourself what you want to do. **You are the Content Guardian for the group and have the authority to determine what your group will cover**.

✓ *Start with something at the time you said you would start:* Icebreaker, what jumped out at them in the lesson, or prayer and the first question.

✓ *Remember to pray before you begin the discussion.* Ask Jesus to teach you what He wants you to learn from the lesson.

✓ *Always read the main Bible passages that are the focus of the lesson.*

Work through the verses in context by paragraphs.

✓ *Ask what grabbed their attention from initial reading.*

✓ *Ask questions about what the text says.* What is happening? What were people thinking and feeling? What truth is presented that corrects specific error in thinking?

✓ *Stay Christ-focused,* emphasizing what He is saying to you through His Word and how you can obey Him and depend upon Him more in your life.

✓ *Decide how to apply what you learned:* in large group, in small groups (2-4), or skipped (personal).

✓ *End on time and with prayer.* Be faithful to end at the time designated for your group. Ask the Lord Jesus to apply in your lives what you learned through His Word.

Practice speaking through your plan as needed.

✓ Read the questions aloud and how you will ask someone to read the Bible verses.

✓ Practice how you will cover the application questions and respond to potential rabbit trails.

✓ Consider how to keep the group members engaged in the study. That will involve an intentional act on your part to resist a lot of "teaching," especially since you have done so much work preparing the study.

Other Resources to Help You Lead a Bible Study Group

BE A CHRIST-FOCUSED SMALL GROUP LEADER

A handbook for leading a women's small group

In this handbook are many more suggestions for managing the discussion, connecting with different kinds of people, dealing with crises that happen to members of your group, and much more. *Be a Christ-Focused Small Group Leader* will answer many of your questions about leading a small group. You can get it from melanienewton.com/shop or from Amazon and most online bookstores.

LEAP INTO LIFESTYLE DISCIPLEMAKING

Take others with you as you follow Christ

This book will show you **what disciplemaking is** and how to do it **in your everyday life**. It includes **thought questions** useful for group discussion as well as **action steps for individuals and ministry leaders**. You can make "lifestyle disciplemaking" a reality for yourself and for your ministry. Leap into lifestyle disciplemaking and take others with as you follow Christ. Get a copy from melanienewton.com/shop or most online bookstores. Watch what God does!

BIBLE STUDY LEADERSHIP MADE EASY VIDEOS

Go to my YouTube channel @joyfulwalking and look for the playlist "Bible Study Leadership Made Easy." These 12 videos cover much of the same information as in this handbook. Checklists referenced in the videos closely match the checklists and worksheets included in this *Bible Study Leadership Made Easy* handbook.

LIFESTYLE DISCIPLEMAKING ARTICLES

Small groups are excellent places for disciplemaking. Go to melanienewton.com/blog. Choose "disciplemaking" category. Read the Christ-focused articles to find out more about disciplemaking and include it in your small group.

LIFESTYLE DISCIPLEMAKING PODCASTS

Listen to Satisfied podcasts "Series 17: Disciplemaking" for more ways to include disciplemaking in your small group.